D1056557

Books by James Tate

The Lost Pilot
The Oblivion Ha-Ha
Absences

Limited editions

Notes of Woe
The Torches
Row with Your Hair
Shepherds of the Mist
Hints to Pilgrims

ABSENCES

ABSENCES

New Poems by

James Tate

AN ATLANTIC MONTHLY PRESS BOOK
Little, Brown and Company — Boston–Toronto

B

T07/72

Some of these poems have previously been published by: *Amphora,
The Antioch Review, Arion's Dolphin, The Atlantic, Black Box,
Brown Bag, Chicago Tribune, Emerson Review,* Halty Ferguson
Publishing Company, *Harvard Advocate, Hearse, The Iowa Re-
view, Kayak, Lillabulero, The Little Review, Mediterranean Re-
view, Mill Mountain Review, Partisan Review,* "Saint John of the
Cross in Prison" originally appeared in *Poetry,* Pym-Randall
Press, *Quabbin, Sumac,* Unicorn Press.

Library of Congress Cataloging in Publication Data

Tate, James, 1943–
    Absences; new poems.

    "An Atlantic Monthly Press book."
    I. Title.
PS3570.A8A63   811'.5'4   72–1057
ISBN 0–316–83237–5

ATLANTIC–LITTLE, BROWN BOOKS
ARE PUBLISHED BY
LITTLE, BROWN AND COMPANY
IN ASSOCIATION WITH
THE ATLANTIC MONTHLY PRESS

*Published simultaneously in Canada
by Little, Brown & Company (Canada) Limited*

PRINTED IN THE UNITED STATES OF AMERICA

For My Mother

Contents

Four

Harm Alarm

I dash into the bush.
I make myself very small.
Then I look quickly
under the bush.
When I am certain
that all harm sleeps
in a cradle
across the ocean,
I hop back on the pavement
and resume my morning walk.
On that other shore
I should be
just about awake now,
slapping myself
every few minutes.

One

Contagion

When I drink
I am the only man
in New York City.
There are no lights,
but I am used to that.
There are the staircases
that go forever upward
like the twisted branches

of a cemetery willow.
No one has climbed them
since prohibition.
And the overturned automobiles
stripped to their skeletons,
chewed clean
by the darkness.

Then I see the ember of
a cigarette in an alley,
and know that I am no longer
alone. One of us
is still shaking.
And has led the other
into some huddle of extinction.

Is There Anything

How about the haycocks sloping down to the sea,
do you want them,
do you want to talk about them?

Once she rode her horse Crispin there.
Hold me tight, kiss me quick, she said,
this room is smaller than a real room.

And then she noticed that she was late
to meet her husband's plane:
she put on her uniform and walked into the sea.

> *Far away, her father slept with a shotgun:*
> *afraid of the gypsies.*

She could not walk fast enough,
nor did she use proper names
in her elegies.

When it started to rain she stopped crying:
she knelt and laid a shilling
at the foot of a boiling rock:

Is there anything you want, it asked,
anything we can do for you?
The water was full of holes

like the head of a trepanist.
I ain't nobody I can't know, she said.
It doesn't suit me.

Breathing

I hear something coming,
something like a motorcycle,
something horrible with pistons awry,
with camshafts about to fill the air
with redhot razor-y shrapnel.
At the window, I see nothing.
Correction: I see two girls

playing tennis, they have no
voices, only the muted thump
of the ball kissing the racket,
the sound of a snowball
hitting a snowman, the sound

of a snowman's head rolling
into a river, a snowman with
an alarm clock for a heart
deep inside him. Listen:
someone is breathing.

Someone has a problem
breathing. Someone is blowing
smoke through a straw.
Someone has stopped breathing.
Amazing. Someone broke
his wrist this morning,
broke it into powder.
He did it intentionally.
He had an accident

while breathing.
He was exhaling

when his wrist broke.
Actually

it's a woman breathing.
She's not even thinking
about it. She's thinking
about something else.

The Distant Orgasm

I am reading:
" 'Huh! promising me a hundred children.' Then she
waits for the God to show what he can do, and Siva (but
it can't be Siva) is touched, and forced by her faith,
resuscitates the husband."
                    And as I am reading
                    I hear a cry: Oooooooo!
                    O God, the heart fails
                    I know it
                    it can happen next door
                    (see *Musée des Beaux Arts*)
                    while you are reading
    "What I am telling here is the story according to
the expression of the group. But the Hindus do not know
how to paint, still less how to carve natural expressions.
That is why I am inclined to think that the woman's
attitude should be a little more respectful."
                    What can I do
                    but lunge from bed
                              the telephone . . .
                    no the moments spent
                    dialing may be her last
                    the kiss of life
                    how does it go?
                    Once I had to try it
                    on a boy he
                    was not dying he was
                    only a cub scout
                    but he could die
                    and I could if

I would
save him if
I was not timid
and I was
how *does* it go!
splayed out
in the bathroom she
was stepping
from the shower she
had no history
her heart was free
of history
I would stay with her
hammer the kiss of life
onto her
hold a mirror
over her lips
                    Ooooooooooo!
She cries again
I am slow closing
the book
"The Hindu does not rush. He is never elliptic.
He does not stand out from the group. He is the exact
opposite of the climax. He never bowls you over. In
the 125,000 verses of the Ramayanas, in the 250,000 of
the Mahabharata there is not a flash."
                    I saw her once only
                    she was not
                    attractive
                    no one would call her
                    beautiful
                    I hear her music at night
                    Haydn
                    she plays when she is alone
                    as she is most nights

a working woman
up at seven
I hear the alarm
I hear her hum
as the coffee perks
as the bath runs
as the radio
softly conveys the news
that has occurred
in her sleep
and now she is going
she has been called
as my grandmother would say
she is crossing over
as the spiritualists say
                    Ooooooooooo!
a third time she cries
it must be terrible
it did not show mercy
with swiftness
I have heard that cry
I "respond" to that cry
as if it were caught
in my throat
                    Ooooooooo yes
she says Ooooooooo yes
I am in the doorway
with one foot raised
the foot stays raised
through the next cry
and the next cry
the foot is becoming
aware of something
the awareness moves
up through the ankle
into the calves

One

Contagion

When I drink
I am the only man
in New York City.
There are no lights,
but I am used to that.
There are the staircases
that go forever upward
like the twisted branches

of a cemetery willow.
No one has climbed them
since prohibition.
And the overturned automobiles
stripped to their skeletons,
chewed clean
by the darkness.

Then I see the ember of
a cigarette in an alley,
and know that I am no longer
alone. One of us
is still shaking.
And has led the other
into some huddle of extinction.

Harm Alarm

I dash into the bush.
I make myself very small.
Then I look quickly
under the bush.
When I am certain
that all harm sleeps
in a cradle
across the ocean,
I hop back on the pavement
and resume my morning walk.
On that other shore
I should be
just about awake now,
slapping myself
every few minutes.

Is There Anything

How about the haycocks sloping down to the sea,
do you want them,
do you want to talk about them?

Once she rode her horse Crispin there.
Hold me tight, kiss me quick, she said,
this room is smaller than a real room.

And then she noticed that she was late
to meet her husband's plane:
she put on her uniform and walked into the sea.

> *Far away, her father slept with a shotgun:*
> *afraid of the gypsies.*

She could not walk fast enough,
nor did she use proper names
in her elegies.

When it started to rain she stopped crying:
she knelt and laid a shilling
at the foot of a boiling rock:

Is there anything you want, it asked,
anything we can do for you?
The water was full of holes

like the head of a trepanist.
I ain't nobody I can't know, she said.
It doesn't suit me.

Breathing

I hear something coming,
something like a motorcycle,
something horrible with pistons awry,
with camshafts about to fill the air
with redhot razor-y shrapnel.
At the window, I see nothing.
Correction: I see two girls

playing tennis, they have no
voices, only the muted thump
of the ball kissing the racket,
the sound of a snowball
hitting a snowman, the sound

of a snowman's head rolling
into a river, a snowman with
an alarm clock for a heart
deep inside him. Listen:
someone is breathing.

Someone has a problem
breathing. Someone is blowing
smoke through a straw.
Someone has stopped breathing.
Amazing. Someone broke
his wrist this morning,
broke it into powder.
He did it intentionally.
He had an accident

while breathing.
He was exhaling

when his wrist broke.
Actually

it's a woman breathing.
She's not even thinking
about it. She's thinking
about something else.

The Distant Orgasm

I am reading:
" 'Huh! promising me a hundred children.' Then she
waits for the God to show what he can do, and Siva (but
it can't be Siva) is touched, and forced by her faith,
resuscitates the husband."

And as I am reading
I hear a cry: Ooooooo!
O God, the heart fails
I know it
it can happen next door
(see *Musée des Beaux Arts*)
while you are reading
"What I am telling here is the story according to
the expression of the group. But the Hindus do not know
how to paint, still less how to carve natural expressions.
That is why I am inclined to think that the woman's
attitude should be a little more respectful."

What can I do
but lunge from bed
the telephone . . .
no the moments spent
dialing may be her last
the kiss of life
how does it go?
Once I had to try it
on a boy he
was not dying he was
only a cub scout
but he could die
and I could if

the knees and into the thighs
the thighs say
this neighbor of mine
is not dying
no she is not dying
the foot lowers itself
to the ground
one foot follows the other
back into the bedroom
the hands pick up
the book
the eyes are shy now
they feel foolish
but they must read
to the end.

Someone must think
she is beautiful.

The Private Intrigue
of Melancholy

Hotels, hospitals, jails
are homes in yourself you return to
as some do to Garbo movies.

Cities become personal,
particular buildings and addresses:
fallen down every staircase
someone lies dead.

Then the music from windows
writes a lovenote-summons on the air.
And you're infested with angels!

A Guide to the Stone Age

for Charles Simic

A heart that resembles a cave,
a throat of shavings,
an arm with no end and no beginning:

How about the telephone?
— Not yet.

The cave in your skull,
a throat with a crack in it,
a heart that still resembles a cave:

How about the knife?
— Later.

The fire in the cave of your skull,
a beast who died shaving,
a cave with no end and no beginning:

A big ship!
— Shut up.

Instructions which ask you to burn other instructions,
a circle with a crack in it,
a stone with an arm:

A hat?
— Not the hat.

A ship with a knife in it,
a telephone with a hat over it,
a cave with a heart:

The Stone Age?
— There is no end to it.

Brainchild

Scientists have injected into rats
a fear of darkness.

How can I fear anything,
I can drive with my lights off
two miles an hour
through a blind intersection
full of rats:

one thin man is scaling a very thin ledge
because he wants a radio.

I don't blame him;
I go faster, turn a corner.

Even my car has its own radio
and darkness
such as can be heard
or imagined when there is nothing
the light has not uncovered
for so many days
my head wants to ache.

They have to boil
eleven pounds of rat brains
to yield less than a thousandth of a gram
of scotophobin —

but that thousandth of a gram
is a fear of darkness so pure,

I hide it in the extreme edges
of a smile, which they are
sure to find some day and bake

into one howling brainchild.

The Boy

A Man does not age, but a boy, a boy,
doubled up and falling down
all-changing unchanging,
on his face as though shot,
shoving his frail boat out into eternity,

and all things become dead,
dead as he knows them,
and the vacuum is his living presence,
very cold as he vacuums
through the cold lamplight,
alone in his room,
and sneezes upon the embers

as though greatly drugged in another movie.
Surely it can't be me
back into time forward
who is vacuuming in his white dress of innocence
into this small place,
I can't go fast enough,

I want to lay myself down on a large platter
of innocence, with my eyes closed,
I flee into the deepest darkest jungle,
unwritten and unwritable
as though in a movie of our fathers
waltzing with the death machine
from a star and it is always

the same, there is no space empty enough
to receive that flower
without sinister glances,
I cannot think of one,
each belongs to another

but I belong to water,
the nights that exist inside the night,

I who have no home have no destination either,
one bone against another,
I carve what I carve
to be rid of myself by morning
by deep dreams disintegrated.

Hidden Drives

I can no longer see behind the tree,
the tree does not rise nor does it bow.
The leaves are leaves,
not tongues or hands.
I wish they were hands.

To tie a string to the leg of an oriole
would be deplorable:
if I were younger I would think it
a fun machine.

Now I'm mystified by history
and statistics — I mean satisfied
with hysterical mysteries.
Sometimes I just get up and break a window
laughing a little or
think about the traveling people.

A bird flies in the library
and dies at my feet,
so I dream of the secret movements
of the local constabulary.

I say "isthmus" out loud — *a narrow strip
of land connecting two larger bodies* —
because I cannot carry my own burdens.
There is no time for confessions,
we agree on that at least.

But there may be more sides to us
than we know: the childhood
with lilies of the valley wobbling
on its hidden grave . . .

I remember hauling a glass of water
around it for hours.

O yes, our lives are going on without us.
O no, we never finish chasing.

Lovelife on the Liffey

Better to stare into this
black face of a river
and know that thirty miles
from here it passes her door.
Once I thought oubliette
meant obfuscate now it is
my place in her heart and
I am happy there.

I bet they don't have any
perfume in that cruel shop
like the perfume she wears:
"I killed a forlorn darkling
beside the coral quays?"
— Never heard of it!
I hear her baching at the
organ when my days are over
(which is another kind
of perfume no one knows).

Quick, climb into the river
and crawl along the floor
to catch a glimpse of her:
sorrow queen in hydrangea
gown: better to die drown-
ing in her miracle cool
eyes than fool the world
without her for a thousand
years.

Wait for Me

A dream of life a dream of birth
a dream of moving
from one world into another

All night dismantling the synapses
unplugging the veins and arteries . . .

Hello I am a cake of soap
dissolving in a warm bath

A train with no windows and no doors
a lover with no eyes for his mask
— inside is the speed of life

Who can doubt the worth of it
each letter written is obsolete
before it finds its friend

Our life is shorter now
full of chaotic numbers
which never complete a day

It will be the same
as it has always been
and you are right to pack

your heart in ice
if you believe this.

The Delicate Riders

I hang my head
on the furniture van
abandoned alongside
an arcaded palace;
alas my woman
is the brand of goose
that cruises through cemeteries
breaking the periscopes
off graves.
I hear a laugh swim up
from the part of myself
I've killed:
those moons
will be there
when I can't even walk.
I know the squalor
of night to night survival,
like the lock of hair
in a dead man's palm.
I place a hanky
over this dream
and wish a trampoline
over her mother's village.
The trees
with their long red hair
dressed in sudden rain
wave a sigh to me —

aphasia smile,
belladonna kiss:
another motionless voyage.
I'll sit down now
and drill a little hole
through this dawnlessness.

If You Would Disappear
at Sea

If you would disappear at sea,
if I would ride a horse over the mountains
from Chile to Mexico . . .

No, we are not in the movies.
I cannot promise you
the red wreaths of promise.

Two rooms watching each other.

The door is everywhere and yet
parenthetical, thankless;
so close to home, no way to get there.

We abandon ourselves, become
invisible, blowing over this

charred field, proud
that we have finished with
the pure amateur's
defensive circling.

My Girl

Those empty (blind) trains
crossing the Alps
are trying to find you

The Indian sisters
dead six months
dream of you
they envy your blue eyes
which have no coverings

And from a fourth dimension
lost husbands
are winding their way back
to woo you
from your solitary days

No the gravediggers
will never uncover you
the scrolls don't mention you
once

The poor seekers
with their red lanterns
so close at times
are waylaid by birdcalls
thunder drums

Their work is endless
your name a wishbone
caught in their throats

A Friend Told Me

You came by
several months after,
at your request,
I'd gone home
to America:
you wanted to talk,
she guessed —
before your dinner party
down the street.
And then you couldn't talk,
"not where we'd been together"
you said, crying
on your pretty dress.

stood there on the step,
snow turning scarlet
on your velvet hat,
wishing a larger pain
would soak you up.

Two

"I'll write a song about nothing at all,
Not about myself, nor about anything else.
Not about love, nor about the joys of youth,
    Nor anything else.
I wrote it just now as I slept
    In the saddle.
I do not know at which hour I was born;
I am not joyful and yet not sad;
I am neither reserved nor intimate
    And can do nothing about it:
I was put under a spell one night
    On a high hill."
        — *Guillaume IX of Aquitaine* (*1071–1127*)

Absences

When did you begin your quest?
I'm late now.
Crucial moment before a shave,
the stars are famished.
Pop off my arms,
give them away, no, throw.
Neither possibility
is a possibility:
putrid sludge of veins and arteries.
I play everything backwards
to see how it will be next time,
such a textbook. All

is suddenly quiet: this legend
has only one knife,
the wind is nothing to me,
it flies in no direction
like a thousand crows,
trips me in my flight of nightness.
Do you want the bones
beneath my eyelid?
I'm late now.

2.

I'm free of that little bit of sunshine.
She has killed me with one cold glance.
I sit back now and wait
for an explosion of larks,
but nothing comes.
Some terrible venom in a stare,
I wish I had one.
Not even hot coals
to carry with me
as I watch the last moth leave.
I existed in the wrong hour of dawn,
that kind of beauty
so no miles from anything.

3.

The eye wants to sleep
but the head is no mattress.
I break the railroad in two.
All the terrifying endless chaotic detail,
worthless narcoleptic wombats.
A dirty comb in the house
of the recently deceased.
No wound there, what is it then?
We are doing what we should
in the barbershop cortege,
a great deal of boring
& irrelevant information.
His age is not known.

4.

In a drunken moment years ago
the hero would be me,
effervescent, welcoming a rattled polka dot
of snow, instead of just sitting here
nervously, twisting a casual wink
into this, in a ditch computing
the future, the dust & the whiteness.
I feel a morbid desire for music.
It comes to zero,
knowing another is near,
a wise man, singing.
Never say drunken angry visionary.
I knit the floating mouth
to the sheep called nobler.

5.

People behaving like molecular structures
with pins in them.
This is what feels best,
as if to say you have grown old
to endless slights of hand.
Yes, ashes fall upward.
You are an extremely ordinary man,
a scarf riding the warm cold wind
in a closet of rags
vampires have abandoned.

6.

He asked for it.
When a clock dies
no one wakes.
Mirthless portals
without moisture.
My dream is a canopy:
if the storm bore malice,
have some tea.
I'm living out a sentence,
trying not to break
the interference of fortune.
Lovers are at a loss now,
surrounded by a brilliant display
representing a palm tree
in fireworks
strangled by curlicues of night;

a mirage of fabulous insects
melting in the ballroom
with the warmth of new love;

and the cigarette in the garden,
watching the cabooseman
toss his handkerchief of salt
into an erotic prairie.

I think I remember myself
poised at the end,

holding something
or pushing something away.
What else could I do?

7.

We should all be behind bars.
I am the commuter
no matter how unreachably far away.
Burrowing a tunnel
through the dump,
please erase sleep from this dream.
Not a tear was shed all spring.
The springs grow shorter.
I hold my breath in my hand.
Why do I bother to speak?
Make love to a moose, maybe.
I can imagine a wife
serving dinner
of light bulbs & garbage cans.
How do you like your mashed potatoes?
With pins in them.
Pretty soon I am talking
to the secretary
of her personal secretary,
a faithful wife, in herself,

a jaspered morning.

8.

So close I came to you
each moment I was alive:
summer of turnstiles,
unnatural waltzes
with funereal jurors.
In the pink lobby
the abortion got away.
Large soft brown disks.
Now it is quiet in the bar:
no one says to the other,
"It is all one to me,
sexuality & the trucking industry."
Break open ourselves,
but there are not enough selves
to go around.

9.

The littlest finger on the left hand
on which so much hangs,
sings his silent serenade.
What are you doing?
Where are you going?
The lightning will sting your eyes.
A particular formation of clouds —
I am not referring to my mother,
the gypsy — is learning to speak:
finer cold I should not have to think.
And now they want back their nothing.
But the few I do have
actually I don't have.

The mattress is disembowelled.
When you call her name, Wanda
falls into a deep sleep,
the littlest finger on her left hand
is mugged by lint.

10.

I was confused
then I got used to it
as I got used to whiskers.
The laugh is bitter & forced,
flat as a hungover Sunday school teacher
all beat-up by the blight
of the truth of the night before.
There, apologize, for thinking.
A pinched and brittle smile.
Throw a handful of magic
purple dust in my eyes
so I can see the last straw.
All the time I am afraid
the children from my childhood
will get me, my whistling
hot fantasy: those were great moments
in somebody's life.

I look at the ceiling,
then turn and avert my eyes,
and say exactly what is expected of me:
the days just come to me.

Why aren't you in my way?

11.

Where do the words go
when I have done with them?
My mouth should chase them.

The moon in her white nightgown,
the moon in her nightgown of nonchalance,
the warm drawers of the moon:

I don't know what I'm going to do
but it will include the terror
of earrings, earrings in the back seat,

nylons on the tub.

12.

I had to move across the street
to get a better perspective.
It feels so good I'm never coming back.
I'm with the graveman in his television
over a missile site in Nebraska.
We treat ourselves
to a pizza; lifelines are concrete
around our last secret.
The center of the earth
is a ravenous magnet,
it's hard work
to keep anything away from it.
In a pile of money
try to fornicate,
she on her knees, etc.
The skydiver rises!
The green ghost
breaks the lamp
filling a common grave,
my only evidence.
All of heaven's little soldiers
enter the rainbow of indifference
& ask to come out
for the purpose of blinding
the fools who pretend they know me.

13.

A child plots his life to the end;
and spends the rest of his days
trying to remember the plot.
To the pure everything is rotten.
I could guess myself blue.
Fish me out of a sunny bottle
a pocketful of mumbles:
we should get started on that
jade bridge, autumn juvenalia
cannot wait. We should make
history exciting (jejune speculation).
O blind nurse of autumn,
texture of cork, breath
of flüglehorn, Ah . . . Mister Jelly!

14.

Life wrapped up in a shoestring,
as I run from room to room.
It changes me as time goes by.
I drive inward
like a rat;
if you hate what you love
or vice versa,
would you burn down a forest
to kill one bear?
All the brouhaha over our survival,
days like ragas: sir the blips
are approaching, the bloats
are groaning.
A world without alps,
like what we've wanted to do
when nobody was around.
Rife with rising roses,
hosanna savanna.

The air crawling out of the tires.

15.

Haggling over the privilege
of sending a rubber stamp to Venus

the rampaging butterflies
cut out Lorca's heart
that has cleaned this planet
in a stolen airplane

I got my chance
very dry and ascetic
idle as a lamb

Tomorrow I will give her
a telescope
with my dates respectively
scratched on each lens

adding a small stone
or taking one away
some in couples
some in threes & fours
populate the desert

16.

A small man from another world said:
people live on gloomily,
come in cars or boats
— hubba hubba would you look at —
while driving to the business conference,
totally air-conditioned,
sitting with a false humility
when a tree dies.

An asterisk in the heart,
at the same time
the difference between them
so you can read it in a mirror
because "there ain't nothin'
you ain't heard" including
a few previews of The Thing,
drenching herself
just when I feel
it isn't cinematic sex,
it isn't built up to.
Independent of the universe.

17.

Thus the galaxy is inhabited
shouting & dancing around
with my ex-girlfriend, the spy.
We had a big fight one night
because she wouldn't wash her hands
of the blood from a coitus
interruptus midnight phone call.
There never vos sich times.
Then I swiftly pierced my Bible
with an icepick &
slept in a field of general blur.
Some particularly dear friend
I can't conceive of
that brings your face to mine,

a well to be filled with
tossed pennies, a pair
of green bikini panties
stranded on the doorknob

is my favorite cave.

18.

I have nothing to stop my brother:
as I try to predict his next move
a girl is blowing suds out the window.
There must be millions.
A postcard in the mud
tinkles with transparent scripture.
Sunshine came down
on the weird statues
out front the hotel
of three worlds: your bag
of tears is all
you have to empty
before you enter.

On the clerk's lapel spells Roxy.

19.

I'll never go that far again.
I'm happy it's over.
What's inside the fiddle in the meadow?
Under the shadow of the hammer
the constant flow
of the great body snatcher
through the chattering streets.
Way back there in the avalanche
following some ship lover
over the horizon
the mean touchiness of creation
hovers unapproachably

like a permanent wink.

20.

Toto, I don't think we're in Kansas.
The orange glow of an erased creature
murdered in comfort by mama's ax
flies into the organ.
The voice of the leaf on the neck
poisons the dowry in the yellow kitchen.
Soft Oothoon, after all, dropped
the wood louse overboard
with a sailor's smile.
And eleven elves drop dead
in the basin of gold trousers.
Prayers lie like pale beards
on the street. Nearing an island,
I forget to wave. It is too beautiful
to excite me with the idea
of accessibility.

Three

South End

The challenge is always to find the ultimate
in the ordinary horseshit why bother

to get in a car and pretend you are going
a different place to live each day as if

in ignorance of each other's desires
betrayals are not counted saturday night

when it was real warm read the paper and fell
off early in a hot flea-infested building

one must pass by the simple objects suitcase
coffee cup tennis shoe to take account of

life which passes by I sit here and stare
watch a ball game or tease the crazy kid

sunday afternoons are worse everything is
closed nobody drops in they all have

families and places to go so I walk
a straight line from this chair to

that table so what I paid fifteen dollars
for that table the dues and still

I'm foiled in every dream some folks
sit out on the front stoop all night

slowly they roll through the dead plum
trees and fill the air with a numbing moan.

My Great Great Etc.
Uncle Patrick Henry

There's a fortune to be made in just about everything
in this country, somebody's father had to invent
everything — baby food, tractors, rat poisoning.
My family's obviously done nothing since the beginning
of time. They invented poverty and bad taste
and getting by and taking it from the boss.
O my mother goes around chewing her nails and
spitting them in a jar: You should be ashamed
of yourself she says, think of your family.
My family I say what have they ever done but
paint by numbers the most absurd disgusting scenes
of plastic squalor and human degradation.
Well then think of your great great etc. Uncle
Patrick Henry.

Rustin Steel Is Driving the Crew
to the River

Rustin Steel is driving the crew to the river. A long
gunmetal Cadillac has stopped in front of him. He tries
the brakes. A little, a little more. He presses the pedal
all the way to the floor: nothing. With both palms he
presses the horn. No sound. Nothing. No horn, no brakes.
He has with him the best crew in twenty years of driving
the crew bus. He pulls the steering wheel right off its
sprocket, and goes flying through the windshield into
the river. He starts paddling toward shore. The crew
is standing on the banks, cheering! Now he straightens
his course and stretches his arms toward Exeter, twenty
miles downstream, his archenemy, his only hope.

Apology for Eating Geoffrey Movius's Hyacinth

It has come to this,
a life of uncalculated passion
for the barely wriggling throb
of the invisible tube of force
that manufactures a laugh
for smothering pentagons,
fructifying useless poems,
and salvaging broken-hearted penguins.

Holy Kansas City, I hold onto
your earlobes
and blaze a trail
through Boston's murky yawn.
Happy to be grown-up at last,
I bathe my feet in rum,
I take off my shirt
and find serial numbers
chewing jagged holes
in my breasts.
As a result, I consider
blowing my nose in my mouth.

Another Palm Sunday has come and gone.
It's always a letdown.
Life's like that:
one day you're Saint James,
the next you're just the girl across the street
trying to think up a name
for a new cereal,
weird little nightmares
of death-colored snowflakes.

I arrived on your doorstep,
a never-ending passion . . .
it has to be

like this

Spent

spend it all,

quickly

the currency is always changing

+   SHELTER   +
embarrassed to not be
a child
——— EATING EVERYTHING
because it moves

because it does not move
fast enough

because you ARE it
and you love yourself
for being IT
You dance
you make love
to the red dog of sunlight

You speak of darkness
the absence of light

the abscess of light

I speak of the absence
of absence

— do not go away
any of you

I WILL marry you, the whole lot . . .

Tomorrow, I trust
this is true

I invite my old age
to testify,
proving
my plans were the worst

I failed everyone

because my "courage"
was *instant sorrow*

Such a word "courage"
a shudder runs through
an empty house

a puff of smoke shoots
from each fingertip

lordy, what changes

is the desire
for grace

I forget each dawn
my raison d'être

Surely the man who started
this poem
is dead

His fingerprints ate at
my throat

But wait!

we boogie-woogie through
a reunion of the terrors,
a decade
slashes its wrist.

A toast!

"If we were not genuinely
interested in orderly, effective,
quick destruction . . ."

Throw me a rope,

     free at last!

I am beginning to grow again,
I see eye to eye with a snail.

I am running toward you.

We are jumping out of windows,
expecting to make friends
with the people whose windows we pass.

I am a drugstore cowboy,
interested in mysticism,
violins and cannibalism.

For offering me a chair
in which to catch my breath,
to recollect my suicide
in tranquility,

     I praise your wife,
her cooking, intelligence and beauty,

your son and daughter,
the impeccable decor
of your terrific house,

your dog's gleaming coat
and fine breath,

the glass from which I drink,

your eternally warm and sympathetic hand
on my shoulder,

I praise the mysterious ways
of the universe

which have allowed us to share
these truly memorable moments
in this starlit spectacle
of holocaust and slumber.

I am sorry I ate your hyacinth,
but it was so cold and lonely.

Finding an Unmailed
Note in the Attic

On a clear day
I can see England
and England can see me.
I would prefer to write
"a month of Sundays!"
or "Mrs. Grundy's
flunky has a glamorous hernia."
Seconal, all
is forgiven:
     "Dear Vinnie
We sure are worried about you
We're always going around here
wondering where you are
or what you're doing
When we got that telegram
we all almost fainted.
     Jimmie sure is cute
he can almost sit up
when he laughs he looks
so cute. I take care
of him a lot.
     I was sick (awful sick)
~~and last night and last night I~~
~~and last night an~~ and yesterday
and the day before I was sick
but I'm not now
     Well have to quit now
             Love ——"
I can see England.
The planes are loaded,
they are never coming back.

As a Child

I hate to go to the sea.
Mother sings as she bundles me up so tight.

Across the white rolling hills,
across the hills we go.

Mother throws her hat into the sea.
I smoke before the fire,

the fire stroking my face gently.

Museum of Animated Nature

You think you are going to work
but you are going to the cemetery.

*   *   *

Why don't you hide? Everybody saw you.

*   *   *

He moved with fear, she with pain.
A perfect ending for the stupid story,
starring James Tate
and his dog Fear.
She never actually appears.

*   *   *

You keep digging the hole
that leads away from the door
through which you can't get
your karma.

*   *   *

They will take you
where you are going,
but they won't let you stay
where you want to be.

*   *   *

Dawn poem. Noon poem. Dusk poem. Midnight poem.
Another day has parked its chariot inside my head.
I should have said *wrecked* its chariot, because the
word "expendable" puts me to sleep.

*   *   *

What we lie on has long ago disappeared.
I can't imagine that.

*   *   *

No talk: but an orchestration of the years,

April, April, April,
a cough, a trophy of fingerprints.

*   *   *

Ur the Poet sits in an Etruscan pub,
looking for something to worship.

*   *   *

The fool is writing about his childhood again.
The only difference is he did not write about it then.

*   *   *

Getting back to poetry — never mind. The sun
is setting and still no poem has brought her back.

*   *   *

By my friends I am considered a sham.
It is as it should be.
They live such a long time.

*   *   *

One poem provides an axis for a lifetime.
It also provides a nail.

*   *   *

At three o'clock in the morning nobody wants
to hear this shit. They just want to listen to music.

*   *   *

If all the strippers that offered me
red BSA motorcycles
were laid end to end . . .

*   *   *

They see it now as never before,
because it is for the last time.
The elevator is stable;
it is the building that moves.

*   *   *

When your dreams are recorded by spiders
nothing is forgotten, even tomorrow.

*   *   *

You think you are going to the cemetery
but you are going to work.

*   *   *

Why are you hiding? Nobody saw you.

Deaf Girl Playing

This is where I once saw a deaf girl playing in a field.
Because I did not know how to approach her without startling
her, or how I would explain my presence, I hid. I felt
so disgusting, I might as well have raped the child, a grown
man on his belly in a field watching a deaf girl play.
My suit was stained by the grass and I was an hour late
for dinner. I was forced to discard my suit for lack of
a reasonable explanation to my wife, a hundred dollar suit!
We're not rich people, not at all. So there I was, left
to my wool suit in the heat of summer, soaked through by
noon each day. I was an embarrassment to the entire firm:
it is not good for the morale of the fellow worker to flaunt
one's poverty. After several weeks of crippling tension,
my superior finally called me into his office. Rather than
humiliate myself by telling him the truth, I told him I
would wear whatever damned suit I pleased, a suit of armor
if I fancied. It was the first time I had challenged his
authority. And it was the last. I was dismissed. Given
my pay. On the way home I thought, I'll tell her the truth,
yes, why not! Tell her the simple truth, she'll love me
for it. What a touching story. Well, I didn't. I don't
know what happened, a loss of courage, I suppose. I told
her a mistake I had made had cost the company several
thousand dollars, and that, not only was I dismissed, I
would also somehow have to find the money to repay them
the sum of my error. She wept, she beat me, she accused
me of everything from malice to impotency. I helped her
pack and drove her to the bus station. It was too late to
explain. She would never believe me now. How cold the
house was without her. How silent. Each plate I dropped
was like tearing the very flesh from a living animal. When

all were shattered, I knelt in a corner and tried to imagine
what I would say to her, the girl in the field. What could
I say? No utterance could ever reach her. Like a thief
I move through the velvet darkness, nailing my sign on
tree and fence and billboard. DEAF GIRL PLAYING. It is
having its effect. Listen. In slippers and housecoats
more and more men will leave their sleeping wives' sides:
tac tac tac: DEAF GIRL PLAYING: tac tac tac: another
DEAF GIRL PLAYING. No one speaks of anything but nails
and her amazing linen.

Two-Hundred-and-One

We both
move so fast
. . to touch
would be

an illusion

There is the photograph of B and there is the photograph
of L and now there is this photograph of D, whom I do not
know. These are the women, these three women, how they do
cry out to be loved, each in her own way, how each has
honed her failures to a very keen and useful edge. O I
have walked that edge nighttime, daytime, all time, I have
balanced there, I have knelt, I have sung 200 songs there,
on that edge, and each song was addressed to WOMAN to WOMAN
to WOMAN. It is always the wrong song, yes that is astonishing,
to sing 200 times the absolutely *wrong* song. I will try
again, for my new picture, for this picture of D, who is
traveling in California with her new songbook. Here is
a song that will never reach her in time:

> The long long long long
> long long long long long
> woolly hair that covers a
> human fetus, it is
> so beautiful, it
> pierces and stabs
> the birthmark
> on the larynx
> of the sheeplike
> doctor, a loss of strength
> also in music
> to cure without easing,

a form of dementia
occurring usually
at puberty
our hands and feet locked
who sailed to California
for gold, listening
to the sounds in her
own body,
a valuable and fine fabric,
which dissolves
another heart,
made by the ancients.

First Lesson

This is a meditation:
a snake with legs,
a one-legged snake,
a snake with wings,
a one-winged snake,
a rat with sparks,
a fiery rat,
a rat that sings,
a star rat,
a horse that explodes,
an atomic horse,
a horse that melts,
an ice horse,
a bee that flies through concrete,
a pneumatic bee,
a bee that lifts buildings,
the world's strongest bee,
a tree that eats the noses off children,
a bad tree,
a tree that grows inward until it is a dot,
a hill of dots that eats lots of children
(you are not meditating).

The Blue Canyon

(for Fred Will)

1.

The way they think of me, radio strangers to you.
I wish I were "departed hastily"
and never come back not even goodbye.
Hair wandering over a book through the body

causing real pain. The blue angel
is of no use now with a terrible twist
of the soul, the trees are bristling
with sparks, I could still see the trees.

To be something different like a brussels sprout
it's as if we were ants so far away
made of charcoal made of dust,
good enough to erase and coming down

if I had not grown up dissolving into
the swan the way they think of me.

2.

Where it is always night with the neighbors,
they have nothing to give, though you are not
the less staring with your eyes closed.
Hand in hand like gasping sponges,

mannequins with secret exterminators
on their way to work. If these stubs
of wrists could start a fire, I'll just
go to bed dirty and get up dirty.

Dragging an enormous leg of something
behind him he slid from doorway to doorway.
I could still see the trees beating
yourself into an insane bloody pulp,

still see your trees these are the same
as we are all full of worms inside.

3.

A butterfly in a far field of buttercups
ball court nobody wants it to end,
with our tops up, rushing and standing still
while a dwarf's dust glistens in the bathtub.

What's in that hole there you are falling down?
The mind on a kite still lost in the skies
too fast for the eye the hills are alive,
and play dead next to a billion wet corpses,

talking about talking trees when their dullness
is malignant. "Someone dear to us,"
suggested Marie, the pages are torn from
my mouth should chase them over

that thought I nearly died for,
this isn't even my chair, knives with arms.

4.

"Be careful," warned Dino, "you are dropping
all the peas into the aquarium,"
in despair over their blue trousers.
Down the street and into the jungle

"I caught you," he cried. See, I'm swimming
out here off the end because a single
hmmmm can magnolia, the years dotted
with drooling cries, hopelessly broken

then he went to the window and after
a few minutes dived into the flower box
over the town sleeping waking tossing
buildings jumping up and falling down,

tree, ants push the basketball I punched
those cows over that hill last night.

5.

Standing out there with his squashed telescope
with Karl Blind and Mrs. Disney Leith,
I don't know if I'll bother to get up
in the swimming pool, the television bites.

They don't have to speak so many words
sitting on a bench feeding those pigeons.
Sardines have been made fun of long enough
and some people just throw up

their hands when the tailor comes over
the mountain, adjusting to eternal silence
as if finding himself face to face
with Edgar Allen Poe in Macedonia

soaking up some kind of obscure stellar grief
"whom" "I" "do" "not" "know".

6.

Now decades are bowling pins for your perfumed revenge
it chews bombs naturally only the world didn't change.
Days passed like years with every song you sang,
in a sensible array of tatters we smoked.

And the swans, the swans are pasted together,
the very sunset in halves hauntingly,
I listened to what you were thinking about
and thumped into a bottomless free fall.

Get in bed and listen to the chicken's head
again and again, our children the little ones,
and the swans are ejected from the lake
suddenly and without notice. First boil

a mirror, then hurl a cow's eye at it,
I broke the dark, gone my day is gone.

7.

Now and for always I kneel down
folded and stashed into high trees
myrtle ashcan zebra everything I love.
With perfect calm I entered

your mouth was grown over
on your meatball the angel
drove the thin line between worlds.
Almost, not quite, transparent

who wants to die come here,
finally blew all the circuits.
With avenues of pleasure
I am not responding to anything.

Enough crying was not enough.
I'm in the birdbath don't come in.

8.

What's on my mind the stork's knee
most ticklish and succulent
is like a word he can speak the whining sounds:
it is gone now, the whole room is swelling.

Rubberducky that part of woman
that has to be going to the store
before it closes with perfect calm:
sexual eggs, I touch you, causing

throbbing jungle hives while you were out.
"How about Sid?" suggested Dino.
"I hate Sid," said Marie. Trousers
float in the harbor, pizzas.

So spring has come to the blue canyon,
it seems "natural" and "pleases me".

Four

The Soup of Venus

This soup is cold
and it needs something
you probably didn't follow
the recipe, you were
in a hurry and wanted
to surprise me.
That was sweet of you
but you forgot
that I don't like
cold soup.
You might try adding
one bay leaf
while you are in there.
The salt is on the table
and I will experiment
with that myself.
The parsley doesn't
taste much but it
does improve
the appearance.
You used to make
such good soup.
I always bragged
about your soup.
I think that's what
originally attracted me
to you, that hot soup
you used to make.
I loved that soup.
Do you still have

that recipe?
Well, this tastes
a little better now,
lukewarm soup
is my second favorite.

The Immortals

None of us have felt good this year:
pus around the eyes,
sores that come and go with no explanation.
But we still believe we will come through it!
I signal this news
by lifting a little finger.

Teaching the Ape to
Write Poems

They didn't have much trouble
teaching the ape to write poems:
first they strapped him into the chair,
then tied the pencil around his hand
(the paper had already been nailed down).
Then Dr. Bluespire leaned over his shoulder
and whispered into his ear:
"You look like a god sitting there.
Why don't you try writing something?"

The Vacant Lot

Two boys come charging over the hill and discover a small
stagnant pond. It is a very small pond, maybe forty-eight
feet in circumference. It could not be more than three feet
deep at its center; still, it is enough to excite them.

It is the first Sunday after school has been let out
for the summer. They are city boys, dressed in blue cotton
trousers and light-blue long-sleeve shirts.

Immediately they get the idea that they could do a little
fishing in this pond. But first it will take some dredging:
three tires mired in the mud, a small icebox, an old furnace
tank, several orange crates, many random boards, part of a
bed, springs, mattress.

They start right in, tugging and slipping and hurling,
barely missing one another's shaggy heads with the flying
debris. There's even an old Christmas tree skeletonizing
beneath the surface which they huff and puff at with piratical
eagerness.

Behind them the playground has been half-bulldozed; it is
impossible to tell for what purpose. And somewhere over
the mounds of rubble there is a transistor radio whirring
and wheedling a popular tune. Also several jets are stacked-
up overhead, making it difficult for the boys to hear one
another.

When the pond is almost empty, and the water level has
sunk a foot-and-a-half, the boys curl up on its dusty battered
edge and stare into the malted glimmer.

The Buddhists Have the Ball Field

The Buddhists have the ball field. Then the teams
arrive, nine on one, but only three on the other.
The teams confront the Buddhists. The Buddhists
present their permit. There is little point in
arguing it, for the Buddhists clearly have the
permit for the field. And the teams have nothing,
not even two complete teams. It occurs to one team
manager to interest the Buddhists in joining his
team, but the Buddhists won't hear of it. The teams
walk away with their heads hung low. A gentle rain
begins. It would have been called anyway, they
think suddenly.

Man with Wooden Leg
Escapes Prison

Man with wooden leg escapes prison. He's caught.
They take his wooden leg away from him. Each day
he must cross a large hill and swim a wide river
to get to the field where he must work all day on
one leg. This goes on for a year. At the Christmas
Party they give him back his leg. Now he doesn't
want it. His escape is all planned. It requires
only one leg.

End of a Semester

I know I will never pass history,
though I can hear the death rattle of a party,
tears full of stickpins
and a tongue of hot wires.
Nobody remembers
what came out of the sea,

her nose broken;
nobody cared about the green diffused light
across her wrist.
Now, ten thousand Americans
die every minute

from an overdose of cough drops.
Does that make kissing a fetish?
Not if you still have
my childhood with you.
I can belch when I want to,
I can smoke a cigar

when I want to . . .
but I know
I will never get through history.
That cloud
is made of wood.

National Motor Inn

They are playing Anastasia,
the last kicks
of an elitist society:
Martini and Manhattan fog
have made all stories
equally convulsive:

"So then he offers her
ten more dollars and . . ."

The wallpaper is a kind
of velvet, scarlet —
haircuts sparkling
beneath the chandelier,
steak and lobster on
BankAmericard, O

a nightmare that is
so precious we will
portion it out over
everyone else's lifetime.

Daisy's Delirium

The young wren carried a rosy ember
in his beak
and placed it in the curls
of a sleeping cow
with a kiss

Death was nowhere
in this wood

A cloud of buttercups
burst open a fence

Down the road
a man in a large silver car
disappeared

Charles the Big Tunnel

The snow coming down onto
your highly polished casket,
I said Charles would have
wanted it to be like this

Well, it'll keep the spiders
out of his eyes, I thought

I went down into the hole
and smoked a cigarette
your daughter threw a hand-
ful of dust on top of me

I closed my eyes and traveled
to China, nothing doing there
so I hurried back in time

to catch you, you big tunnel,
you percolator of zeros.

Entries

When I think no thing is *like* any other thing
I become speechless, cold, my body turns silver
and water runs off me. There I am
ten feet from myself, possessor of nothing,
uncomprehending of even the simplest particle of dust.
But when I say, You are *like*
a swamp animal during an eclipse,
I am happy, full of wisdom, loved by children
and old men alike. I am sorry if this confuses you.
During an eclipse the swamp animal
acts as though day were night,
drinking when he should be sleeping, etc.
This is why men stay up all night
writing to you.

Saint John of the Cross in Prison

Browsing among the zero hours,
and where I went from there . . .
diabolical? No. I went out
of myself into . . . I did not go
out of myself into the after-

noon of parrots; I did not go out
of myself into the dew; I did
not go out of myself into the
bat-terrors. I did not say silence,
I said nothing about the love I

did not go out of myself into.
I said nothing fire, I said nothing
water, I said nothing air. I went
out of myself into no, into
nowhere. I was not alone.

For a Dying
Philosopher

The swallows slide
from the olive trees
into the poppy-eyed
field, as if on wires.
Leone Vivante has been
reading Dante in his
Sienese garden
for hours. Sapped
of all strength,
melancholy, confused —
no bouquet
is small enough
to amuse him.

The Seeing-Eye People

We harnessed ourselves
up & lumbered around
the mountainside
like a lumber mill with
a headache from too
many buzz saws

We were see-through
people but also
had enough depth
to fall more
or less forever

Most of our furry
friends had lost
their sparkle
blind little prickly
fellows THE DOGS
we called them
born blind not
knowing a snowcapped
mountain from a
swinging door and

We led them by
dragging them through
terror then beauty
turn about with
the off chance that
we The Seeing-Eye
People might know
one from the other

And lend them
the courage as their
kind has so often
lent us to awaken
each day to the
impenetrable darkness
and still find
an excuse to jump

from one grave into
another.

A Death to Death

A grub called DEATH at the center of the earth
is directing traffic.
O god bless the child that forgets
his own death,
    a death to death,
      a breath to death,
        a breath to breath.
This death is tiring, be sure
it will last all day.
A death that comes out of the ocean
and rolls across the continent, gathering friends.
A death hollow at the center, a bronze death.
Cold death on a stick.
A freight train of small but good deaths,
no matter, no matter, no matter.
The death of a shoe,
away with you.
On a windy day
death is a bird without legs.
A death like every other death,
so cruel to say.

Snuffing Out a Candle

Yes, there are warps in the air
in pursuit of something,
weepers how they hypnotize!

And then a shadow speaks to me:

"How do you do?
Was that your footprint
I saw in the sand this morning?"

When It Has Done
with Us

The death's-head moth
gliding over the pond now
like the black grave
of stillness
made beautiful

heals my face
of red windows and running webs

Forest

A man is lost in a harpsichord of light.
On all fours he watches a mushroom grow.

Now it is the sixth night.
He is drinking at a stream,
his face is dun in the moonlight.

Through the still, fanned fronds
he sees an upright man approaching.
He tries to stand but the man
walks over him.

Morning: a greenfinch
and a long-tailed tit.

Night: through the silent fronds
a man on all fours stares
at a man on all fours.

Now it is the first night.

Five

Cycle of Dust

1.

Brushfires all around;
I always say that is living.

And stop abruptly to stare
in terror
at the block of ice.

The tentative colors
shrink inward,
a lilac is stuffed into the air;

the last leaves of night
are ripped out
of this blind world

by a still breeze.

2.

The strollers are one
unending stroller

all Spring on the tip
of a budless branch

They drink slumped over
in the dark
grazing the cold teeth
of the chisel

Then you are no virgin

a little maple leaf
on a chain
sparkles his stardust
on a stranger

3.

Men get down on their knees
and search the toy river

it is daytime
the carnation is bubbling

the owls are sleeping
on a distant black planet

A scarf is pulled quickly
through the veins

of a covered bridge

4.

Feeding those pigeons
each spoonful of stone

eyes of a doe
when nobody was around
say in an empty subway
after midnight

like a baby on fire

kicked off the edge

to indicate
there was no sign
or wise man singing

a buoy of blood
is tossed
to the far shore

5.

Little hands were sprouting
in the cracks
of the sidewalk

they have been told nothing

a champion of kisses
somewhere writing
my own filthy epitaph

that famous
limp grey ray
of light

jackknifes midword
into a world without alps

but I have no feathers, he said

6.

When you put on your nightgown
to get off the ground
the smoke twirls

in amber telephones

Chiaroscuro of fossils
and diving birds

the way I run
from their embrace

into a foreign political paper
tattooed
on a false virgin's cunt

The bazookaman chimed
the first kite of
the day — blindfold the birds

in slippers of secondhands

7.

How it will be next time
on the corner
of asylum street

a woman draped over a balcony
in the sky

a poor fiery
oasis
like the candle revealed

in an autopsy
where the vegetables

cry out
on wolf pit road

in the vertebrae of
her bright malaise

the night was clocked
bodies became
covered with dust

they looked like statues

8.

With a bloody eye
the egg slid from memory:

don't drop your tooth
in the delta,
old evil dead over there.

Change of chair was
an illusion,

pins in them,
as if to say
they are building a guitar

with strings of milk
for the dog to practice
in his whiskey —

from here to there
I'll never go

destroying the desert

9.

Afternoon with a random
stranger in a random

taxi gone down
the drain
in his bathtub,

solitude unfurls
his ribbon

of black light
with the same

savage smile,

perfumed snatches
of a neighbor's party
before

the imaginary
swimming pool,
beneath which

a solitary maggot
the keeper of the keeper

no nothing nothing
at the mercy

of invisible ink.

R2